Ninjo Life Hacks

Journal

for kids

Pictures by
Jelena Stupar
& Rebecca Yee

by Mary Nhin

This book is dedicated to my children— Mikey, Kobe, and Jojo.

This Journal Belongs to:

_____

My Journal Partner is:

_____

What is the Ninja Life Hacks Journal?

This journal allows you to practice the ninja life hacks presented in our books. By practicing the methods and techniques, it will help you develop:

- ⇨ Compassion
- ⇨ Gratitude
- ⇨ Positivity
- ⇨ Honesty
- ⇨ Growth mindset
- ⇨ Fiscal fitness
- ⇨ Courage
- ⇨ Patience
- ⇨ Grit
- ⇨ Empathy

- ⇨ Organizational skills
- ⇨ Kindness
- ⇨ Decision-making skills
- ⇨ Humor
- ⇨ Hope
- ⇨ Communication skills
- ⇨ Inclusion
- ⇨ Diversity
- ⇨ Focus

How do you use the Life Hacks Journal?

Pick a time each day to write in your journal.

Find a journal partner.

Read the stories in the Ninja Life Hacks books series.

Table of Contents

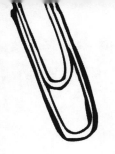

10. Growth Mindset

11. Money

12. Patience

13. Diversity

14. Courage

15. Organization

16. Calm

17. Effort

18. Confidence

19. Focus

20. Inclusion

21. Communication

22. Hope

23. Humor

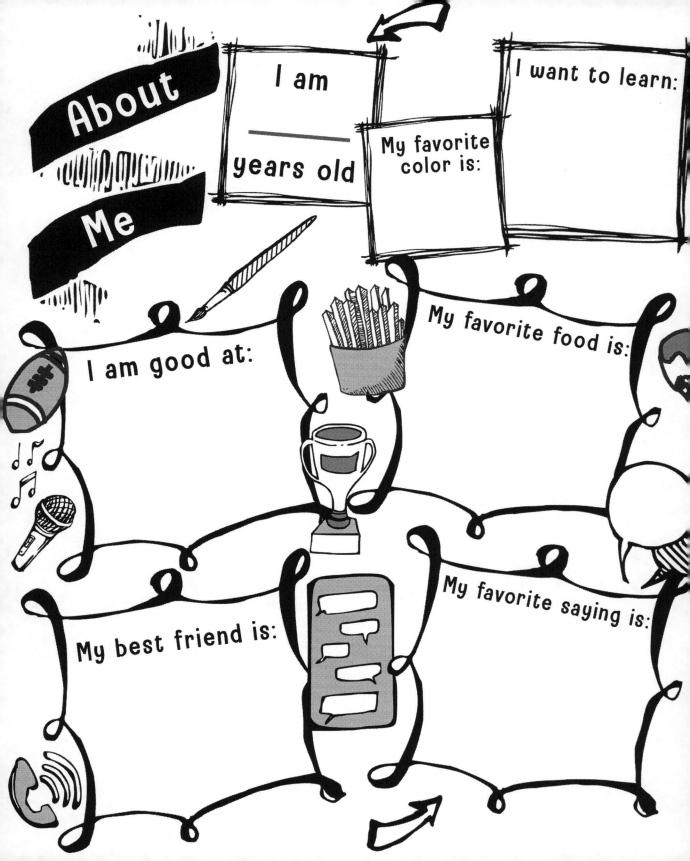

This is what makes me unique:

Circle the sentences that describe you.
Underline those that you would like to be.

I am kind.

I am confident.

I am grateful.

I am focused.

I am wise

I am organized.

I communicate well.

I am inclusive.

I am hopeful.

I am funny.

I am compassionate.

I am calm.

I am courageous.

I am positive.

I am gritty.

I care for the earth.

I am mentally tough.

Challenges help me grow.

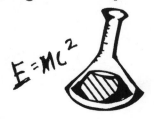

E=MC²

Grit and Mental Toughness

Chapter 1

The

mind

is

stronger

than the

body.

List or draw four things that you continued to try even though they were hard.

Backpacking

Drawing trees

Having mental toughness allows us to overcome obstacles. When the going gets tough, grit allows us to not give up and focus until we reach our goals. How do you develop grit?

There are 4 tools that allow you to grow your grit. The grit strategy is called the 4 Cs:

4 Cs	Tool
Capable	Goals
Calm	Positive Mantras
Carefree	Minimizing
Confident	Visualization

Example	Your Example
I will practice 30 minutes a day, 4 times a week.	List your goals and how you will achieve them.
I can do this!	List your mantra here:
What's the worst thing that can happen?	Answer the question.
I am confident when I visualize my success.	Now close your eyes and visualize your success.

Self-Care and Self-Love

♡♡♡

Chapter 2

We can't
pour
from an
empty
cup.

List or draw five things that always bring a smile to your face.

What are some worries or fears you can let go of today?

Go outside and squint at the sun.

Close your eyes.

Take ten deep breaths.

Gratitude

✿ ♥ ✿

Chapter 3

Happy people are those who are grateful.

List or draw all the things you are grateful for.

Gratitude walk
and
Scavenger Hunt

Go on a nature walk and marvel at Earth's bounties. Look around and take in all that you are grateful for. Then, draw or list them here:

Color in the things you are grateful for about yourself:

- ❤ My health, so I can swim and climb a mountain.

- ❤ My arms, so I can stretch.

- ❤ My legs, so I can run.

- ❤ My teeth, so I can chew food.

- ❤ My ears, so I can hear.

- ❤ My skin, so I can feel.

- ❤ My heart, so I can live.

Kindness

Chapter 4

It costs **nothing** to be **kind.**

Color in where you fall on this scale:

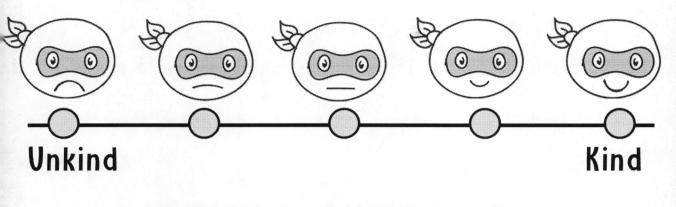

Unkind   **Kind**

Write down one kind thing you did for someone else in the past twenty-four hours.

Kind Ninja loves being caring and compassionate. But it was not always like this. It used to be more about "me, me, me.". Until one day, his heart changed.

Here are some things he did to change things around and be more kind to everyone and everything around him:

Pick up trash.
Help with chores.
Water the plants.
Help the elderly.
Take out the trash.
Say thank you and please more.

What are some things you can do to practice kindness? List or draw them here.

Positivity

Chapter 5

Be the
energy
you want
to
attract.

How do you change these negative thoughts to positive ones?

I can't do that.

_____

I'm not good at this.

_____

I don't think I'll be good.

_____

I'm not doing this right.

_____

What *positive* words can you say to yourself?

Place your hand down below and use your
other hand to trace it's outline.

Write "I believe I am" in the center of the outline, then
write a positive word that describes you on each finger!

Unplugged

Chapter 6

It's bad for your
brain
NOT
to
unplug.

Color in ten places on this world map you'd like to visit.

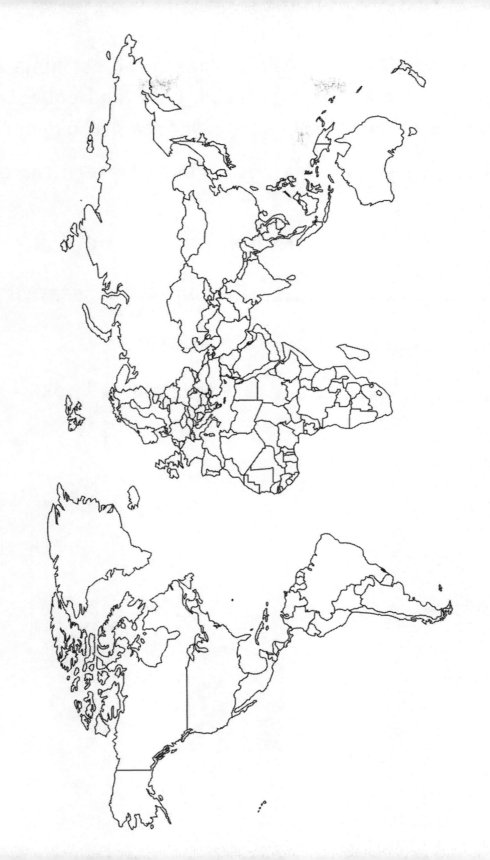

Unplugged Ninja was the calmest, coolest ninja around. But he wasn't always so calm, cool, and collected. He used to suffer from a bit of screen attachment.

Do you know the strategy he used to turn things around:

Fill in the blank with the 3 Rs:

_____with something creative or active.

_____with nature.

_____with music or a book.

KEEP CALM AND STAY COOL

What would you do to unplug?
List or draw them here:

Emotions

Chapter 7

Control your
emotions,
DON'T
let them
control
you.

Things that make me happy	Things that make me mad	Things that make me anxious

What are 5 worries you could live without? Imagine yourself blowing them away once you've written them down.

_____

_____

_____

_____

_____

Color in this spectrum with all the emotions you have experienced.

Anger	anxiety	STRESS
Positivity	LOVE	grumpy
JOY	shy	CALM
fear	HOPE	Compassion
Grateful	sadness	BRAVE
shame	Irritation	lazy

Environmentalism

Chapter 8

What
we
save,
saves us.

Go outside and step on the grass with your bare feet. How does it feel?

How many living things can you find? List or draw them here.

Earth Ninja shows us how one little ninja can make a difference in the world by practicing three simple life habits:

Reduce
Reuse
Recycle

Circle the items in your house you can reuse, recycle, or reduce.

Honesty

Chapter 9

Honesty

is the

best

policy.

-Benjamin Franklin

When was a time you could've lied but you chose not to?

Dishonest Ninja didn't think he was hurting anyone when he chose not to tell the truth.

But what he didn't understand was that each time he lied, he was hurting someone. Because when he told a lie, it changed HIM just a little bit each time.

He changed when he realized that lying made him feel bad inside. It ultimately hurt him by making him feel anxious, worried, and afraid.

Where do you fall on the honesty spectrum?
Put an **X** where you are now and
an **O** where you want to be.

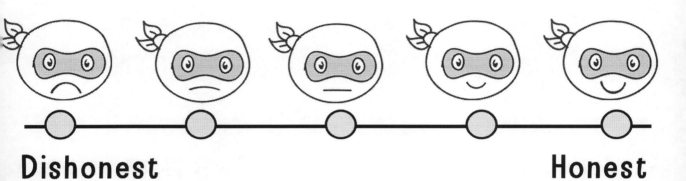

Dishonest   **Honest**

Growth Mindset

Chapter 10

Mistakes help your brain grow.

CHART

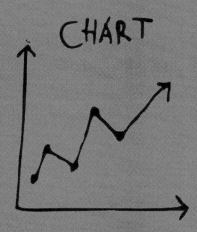

What else helps your brain grow?

Moving
What's your favorite sport?

Sleeping
What do you like doing right before bed?

Learning
What's a new thing you recently learned to do?

Eating
What's your favorite food?

Perfect Ninja must do things perfectly. When his own expectations aren't met, he becomes frustrated and ends up breaking down, crying, or giving up.

But everything changes one day when a friend shows him that mistakes and failures are the best teachers to help us learn and grow.

What I want to do	What others will think	What will I do about it

Money

Chapter 11

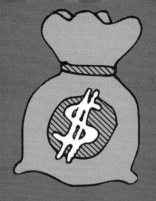

Some people

are so

poor,

all they

have is

money.

What are some things you would do if you had all the money in the world? List or draw them here.

Money Ninja said that money is not just to spend, but you can also save, invest, and donate. He saves his money in the bank and his piggy bank. He invests in several small businesses—his lemonade stand, candy machines, and a YouTube channel.

But of all the things he can do with money, his favorite way to use it is to donate it to charity because it makes him feel good.

Circle the things you value most:

Buying new stuff	Friendship	Clothes
Family	Nature	People
Knowledge	God	Laughter
Books	Earth	Trophies
Love	Shoes	Helping others

Do you have any business ideas?
List or draw them here:

Patience

Chapter 12

Patience is the **calm acceptance** that things can happen in a **different order** than the one you had in your mind.

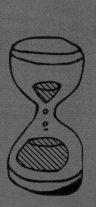

Put an **X** where you fall on the patience scale and an **O** where you want to be.

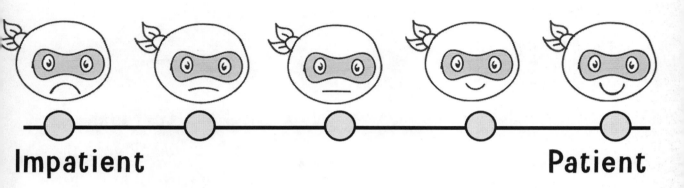

Impatient   **Patient**

Patient Ninja used to be very impatient until he learned how to be more patient. One of his favorite tools to use is to:

Think through the consequences.

What are some things you can be more patient about?
List or draw them here:

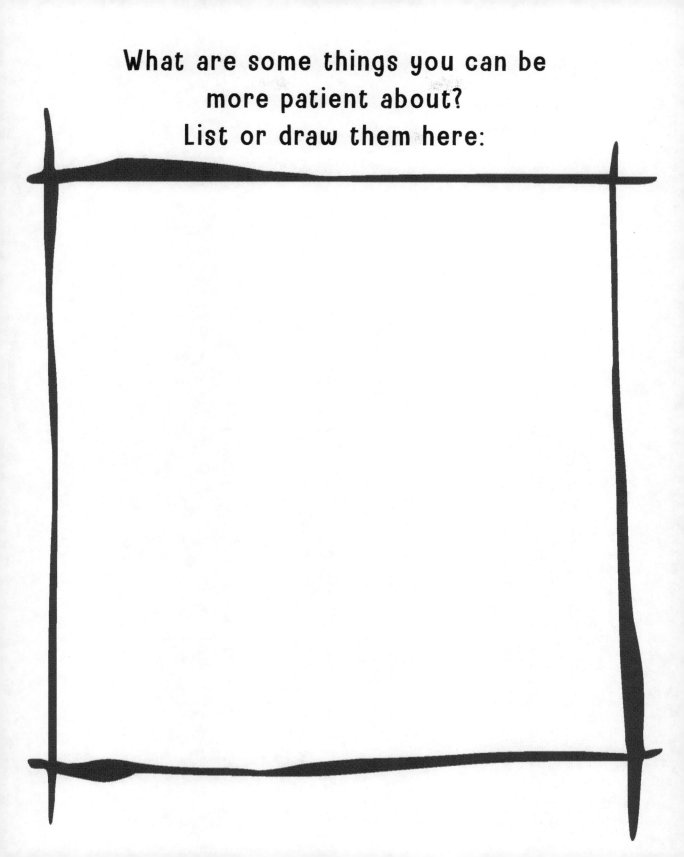

Diversity

Chapter 13

In diversity lies
beauty
and
strength.

Diversity Ninja shows us that regardless of differences in race, gender, ability, background, clothing, language spoken, or skin color, we are all part of the human race.

Do you know someone who is different? List or draw them here.

How are you and this person the same?

I am unique.

This is what makes me unique.
Make a list below.

Draw yourself below wearing a fun and unique outfit.

Courage

Chapter 14

Fear

is a reaction.

Courage

is a decision.

-Sir Winston Churchill

Fill in these three lion outlines with three of your biggest fears, then color them in until you can't see the fear anymore.

Brave Ninja was the bravest ninja in the world. But he wasn't always like this. He used to be scared to speak up or do things he wanted. So he practices the B-R-A-V-E method to become more courageous.

Breathe by taking a few deep breaths.

Relax your muscles.

Adopt positive body language.

Visualize your success.

Embrace a mantra.

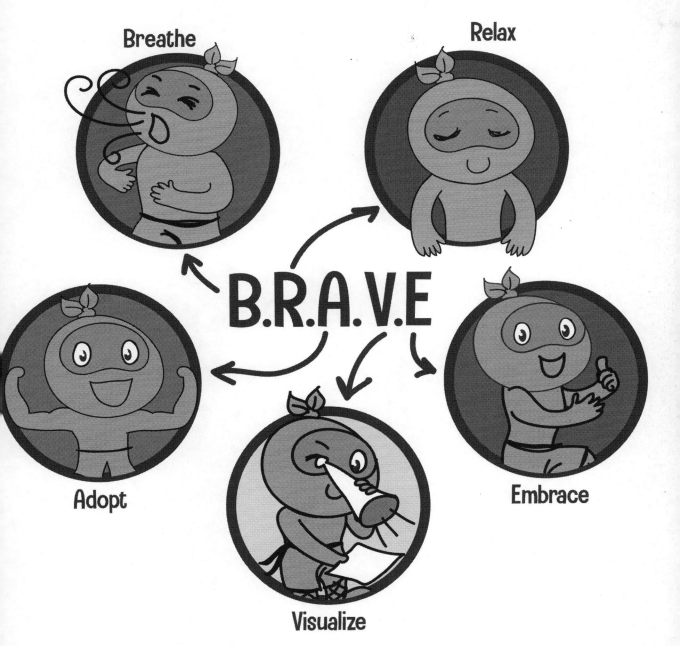

Organization

Chapter 15

Being organized can help your life by making it simpler.

Draw an **X** where your organizational skills are now and an **O** where you want to be.

Unorganized

Organized

Organized Ninja used to be messy until he's introduced to the Cs:

Checklists
Collections
Categories

Do you collect anything? Draw or list it here.

Look around your home. Is anything categorized? List or draw it here.

Calm

Chapter 16

Your
calm
is your best

weapon against
ALL
of your

challenges.

Rate your calmness on this scale.

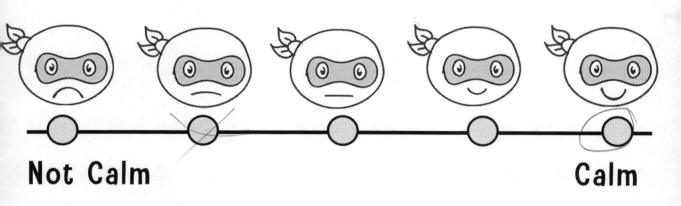

Not Calm   **Calm**

Calm Ninja Yoga Poses

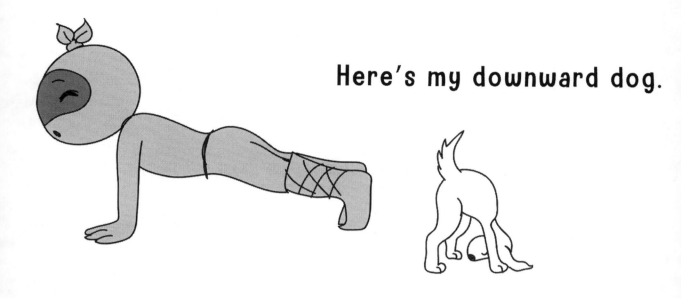

Here's my downward dog.

I can slither like a cobra.

I am brave like a warrior.

I am strong like a boat.

I am as powerful as a lion.

Effort

Chapter 17

Our greatest **weakness** lies in giving up. The most certain way to **succeed** is always to try just one more time.

-Thomas Edison

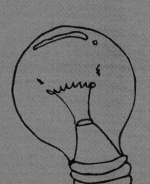

Hard work beats talent when talent doesn't work hard.

What do you think this means?

Smart Ninja excelled at many things. But when things became to hard, he got discouraged easily.

He learned a strategy that helped him overcome challenges. Do you know what the method is called? Write it down here. _____

_____

_____

_____

Think of a problem you are having. How can you handle it? How can you best approach it with a growth mindset?

Confidence

Chapter 18

No one can make you

feel *INFERIOR*

without

your

consent.

-Eleanor Roosevelt

Draw yourself on the mountain. Imagine what you could accomplish if you had no fear.

Confident Ninja learned how to achieve more confidence by practicing the Confidence Code.

The Confidence Code contains two parts:

Picture yourself succeeding.
Practice failing.
Put your goals down on paper.

My Goal Rocket

Write your BIG GOAL here:

Write the steps needed to achieve your goal.

Step 1

It is easier to work toward your big goal when you break it down into smaller steps.

Step 2

Step 3

I reached my goal!

Focus

Chapter 19

Focusing

is about

saying

No.

-Steve Jobs

We all need focus to achieve.
Where are you on the focus scale:

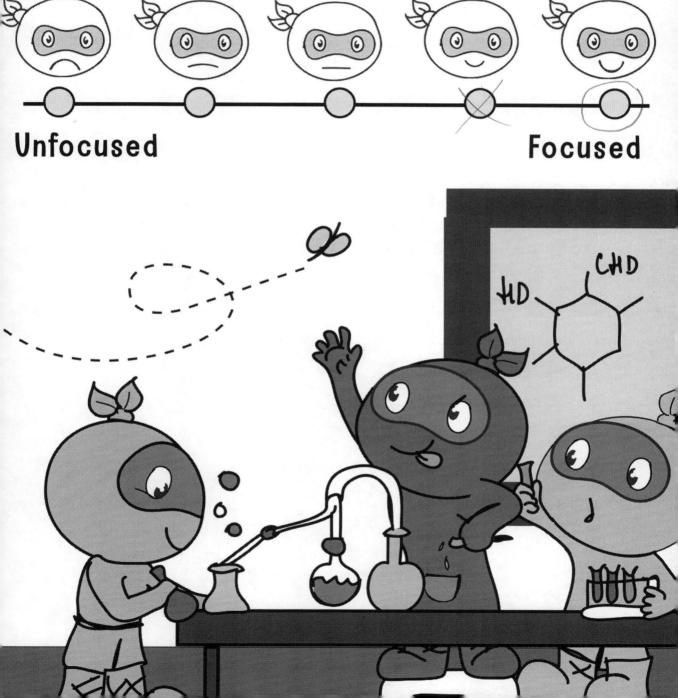

Unfocused

Focused

Focused Ninja shares that even if we aren't born with amazing focus (many of us aren't), we can learn to become more focused by using the F.O.C.U.S. method:

Find distractions and eliminate them.

Organize.

Choose greens and healthy foods.

Use exercise to give your brain a boost.

Split up large assignments into smaller tasks

How do you stay organized?

How do you limit distractions?

What greens and healthy foods do you eat?

Which tasks do you divide up into smaller ones?

Inclusion

Chapter 20

Diversity

is being invited

to the party;

inclusion

is being asked to dance.

-Verna Myers

Practicing inclusion means you intentionally seek to include everyone, no matter their skin color, beliefs, religion, gender, clothing, language they speak, or background.

List or draw one way you've been inclusive.

Developing compassion is the best way to practice inclusion. Compassion begins with putting ourselves in another person's shoes to see how they feel.

How do you feel when you are being compassionate?

Draw or list it here.

Communication

Chapter 21

Communication works for those who work at it.

-John Powell

Learning how to talk and listen are some of the most important life skills.

On a scale of 1 to 10, rate yourself
on your communication skills,
with 10 being the best.

1 2 3 4 5 6 7 8 9 10

On a scale of 1 to 10, rate yourself
on your listening skills,
with 10 being the best.

1 2 3 4 5 6 7 8 9 10

Communication Ninja used to struggle with communicating his emotions and feelings, but then he learned a strategy that helped him blossom into a wonderful communicator.

In the lines below, what method does Communication Ninja use to improve his communication skills?

_____

_____

_____

_____

Think of a time when you really, really listened when the other person was talking and you could you feel their emotions.

How did it make you feel?

Sad

Angry

Happy

Proud

Hope

Chapter 22

Once you **CHOOSE** **hope,** anything's **possible.**

-Christopher Reeves

Go outside at night and look up into the sky, up at the stars.

Make a wish and draw or write it down here:

Draw or write down your *biggest* dream.

Things I want to be	Why I want to be them

Humor

Chapter 23

Humor

is mankind's

greatest

blessing.

-Mark Twain

Here are some funny jokes.

Why are teddy bears never hungry?
They're always stuffed!

What did the policeman say to his tummy?
Freeze. You're under a vest.

What does one volcano say to the other?
I lava you!

What do kids play when they can't play with a phone?
Bored games.

What game does the sky love to play?
Twister.

Why do we never tell jokes about pizza?
They're too cheesy.

Did you hear the joke about the roof?
Never mind, it's over your head.

What time is it when people are throwing pieces of bread at your head?
Time to duck.

What's the difference between a guitar and a fish?
You can tune a guitar, but you can't tuna fish.

What did the sink say to the potty?
You look flushed!

What's a snake's strongest subject in school?
Hiss-tory.

Can you make up your own?
Write them here.

Think of a funny moment in your life. Draw a comic strip about it.

"Why was 6 afraid of 7?" asked Inclusive Ninja.

"I dont know," replied Diversity NInja.

"Because 7, 8, 9," said Inclusive Ninja and they both laughed hysterically.

Self- belief
coloring pages

I believe in myself!

When the going gets tough, I get tougher.

I can be anything I want to be.

I am
brave.

I am PATIENT.

I am Hopeful.

I am GRITTY.

Visit us at GrowGrit.co for fun, free printables.

📷 @marynhin @GrowGrit
#NinjaLifeHacks

f Mary Nhin Grow Grit

▶ Grow Grit

Made in the USA
Columbia, SC
31 May 2022